It's Not Catching

Broken Bones

Heinemann Library
Chicago, Illinois

Angela Royston

Designed by Dave Oakley, Arnos Design
Artwork by Tower Designs UK Ltd and Nick
Hawken
Originated by Dot Gradations Ltd
Printed and bound in China
by South China Printing Company

08 07 06 05 04
10 9 8 7 6 5 4 3 2 1

**Library of Congress
Cataloging-in-Publication Data**
Royston, Angela.
  It's not catching broken bones / Angela Royston.
     v. cm.
Contents: What is a broken bone? -- Who gets
broken bones? -- Twisting your ankle -- Falling --
Serious accidents -- Sprains -- Dislocated joints --
Broken bones -- Treating an injured joint --
Treating a broken bone -- How a broken bone
mends -- Getting strong again -- Preventing
accidents. ISBN 1-4034-4822-1 (hbk.)
  1. Bones--Wounds and injuries--Juvenile
literature. 2. Fractures--Juvenile literature. 3.
Joints--Wounds and injuries--Juvenile literature.
[1. Bones--Wounds and injuries. 2. Fractures. 3.
Joints--Wounds and injuries.] I. Title: Broken
bones. II.
Title.
  RD101.R75 2004
  617.1'5--dc22

                              2003019814

Acknowledgments
The author and publishers are grateful to the
following for permission to reproduce copyright
material: p. 4 Rubberball Productions; pp. 5, 8, 9,
10, 11, 20, 21, 27, 28, 29 Phillip James
Photography; p. 6 Alamy/Image100; p. 7
SPL/Custom Medical Stock Photo; p. 12
Powerstock/Robert J. Bennett; p. 13 Getty
Images/VCL/Spencer Rowell; p. 15 The Wellcome
Trust; p. 16 SPL/Dept. of Clinical Radiology,
Salisbury; p. 17 SPL/Dr P. Marazzi; p. 18, 22 John
Walmsley; p. 19 SPL/Scott Camazine; p. 23
SPL/Jim Selby; p. 25 Trevor Clifford; p. 26 SPL/CC
Studio.

Cover photograph reproduced with permission of
Corbis.

The publishers would like to thank David Wright
for his assistance in the preparation of this book.

Every effort has been made to contact copyright
holders of any material reproduced in this book.
Any omissions will be rectified in subsequent
printings if notice is given to the publisher.

Contents

Some words are shown in bold, **like this.** You can find out what they mean by looking in the glossary.

What Is a Broken Bone?

Bones are the hard materials inside your body that make up your **skeleton.** Bones give your body its shape. They also hold up your head and other parts of your body.

Bones are strong, but sometimes a bone can crack or break. When a bone is **injured,** it is too painful to move properly or to put your weight on.

Who Gets Broken Bones?

Anyone can break a **bone.** People who are very active or are not careful when playing are more likely to have an **accident.**

Bones become more **brittle** as people get older. **Elderly** people, especially women, can easily break a bone. But broken bones are not catching.

Twisting Your Ankle

When you are running and playing, it is very easy to twist your **ankle.** Your ankle might suddenly give way, or you may twist your foot as you jump and land the wrong way.

Twisting your ankle is not usually serious, and the pain soon goes away. But if your ankle swells up, you may have **sprained** it or even broken a **bone.**

Falling

When you fall, you can hit and **jolt** a **bone.**
A bad jolt can crack or break the bone.

Falling on a hard surface, such as **concrete,** will jolt your bones. Falling off somewhere high above the ground jolts your bones, too.

Serious Accidents

Sometimes people are involved in bad **accidents** such as car crashes. Sometimes people are killed in car crashes. Others may have one or more **bones** broken.

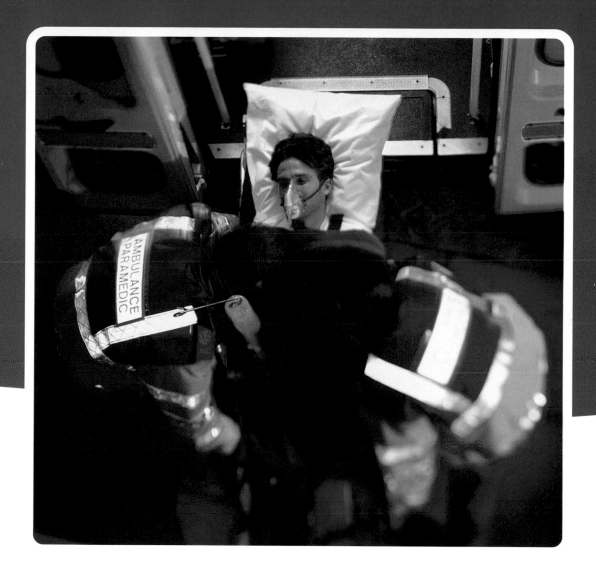

Being run over is another kind of bad accident. Being hit by a moving car or other vehicle is likely to break a person's bones and hurt that person very badly.

Sprains

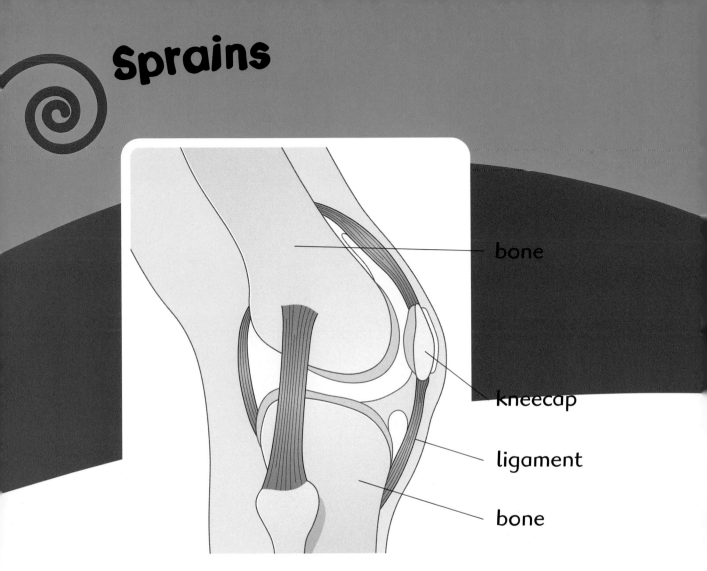

bone

kneecap

ligament

bone

A **joint** is where two or more **bones** meet. **Ligaments** are stretchy bands that hold the joint together. A joint is **sprained** when a ligament is torn or stretched.

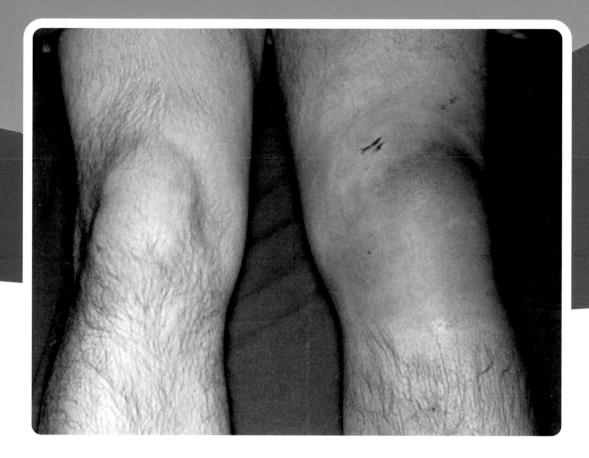

When a ligament is damaged, the joint can be very painful. It quickly becomes swollen. Trying to move the joint can make the pain even worse.

Dislocated Joints

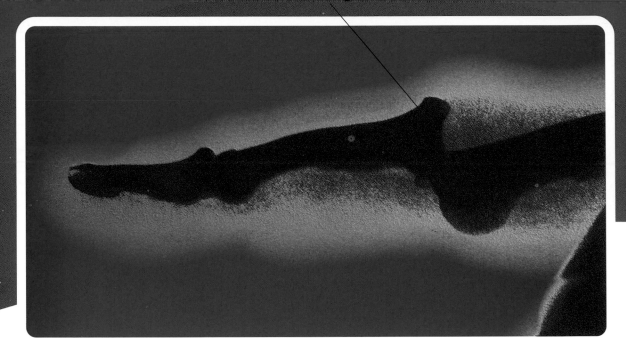

dislocated joint

In a **joint,** the ends of the **bones** fit together. In some **accidents,** a bone is pulled out of position. This means the bone is **dislocated.**

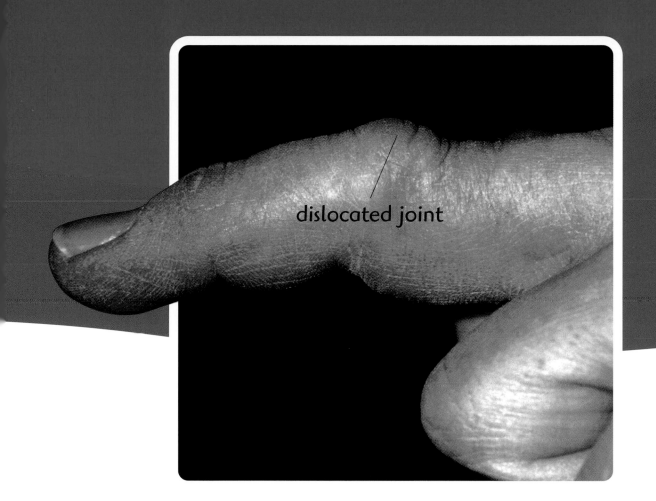

dislocated joint

You can sometimes tell if a joint is dislocated because its shape looks wrong. The joint can be very painful to move or to touch.

Broken Bones

An **accident** can crack a **bone** or break it all the way through. Only an **X ray** can show where and how a bone is damaged.

broken bones

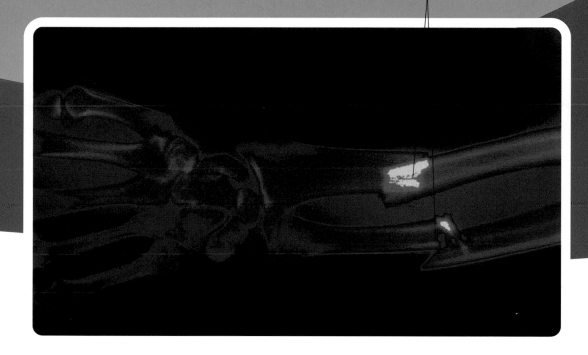

An X-ray machine takes a picture of the **injured** bones. This X ray shows a person's arm. It shows that two of the bones are broken.

Treating an Injured Joint

The best treatment for a **sprained joint** is to rest it while the **injured ligament heals** itself. A stretchy bandage can help to support the joint while it heals.

If a joint is **dislocated,** a doctor will move the **bones** back into the right position. As the joint gets better and stops hurting, you should exercise it gently. This boy is circling his foot to exercise his **ankle.**

Treating a Broken Bone

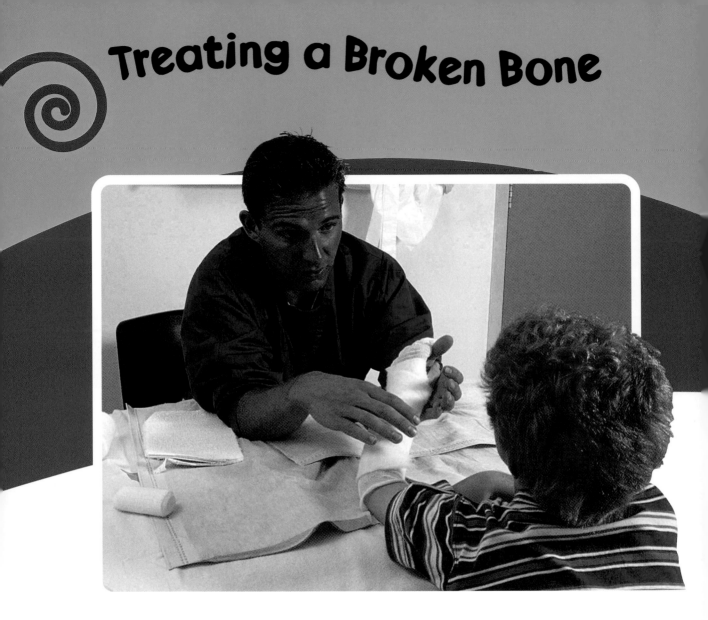

A broken **bone** needs to be kept still while it **heals.** First, the doctor puts the bone back in the correct position. Then, a wet bandage is wound around it.

22

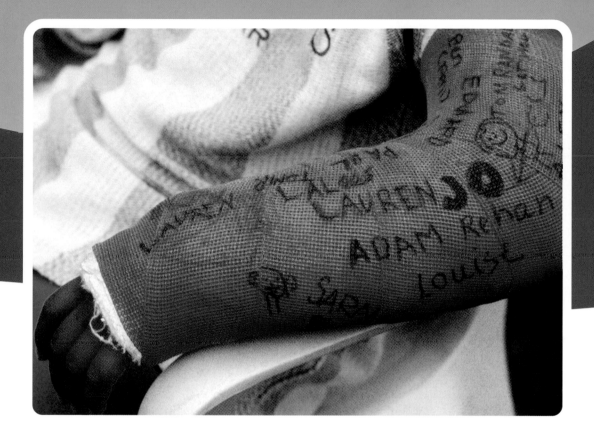

The bandage contains a special substance. As the bandage dries, the substance hardens. It forms a strong **cast** that protects the bone.

How a Broken Bone Mends

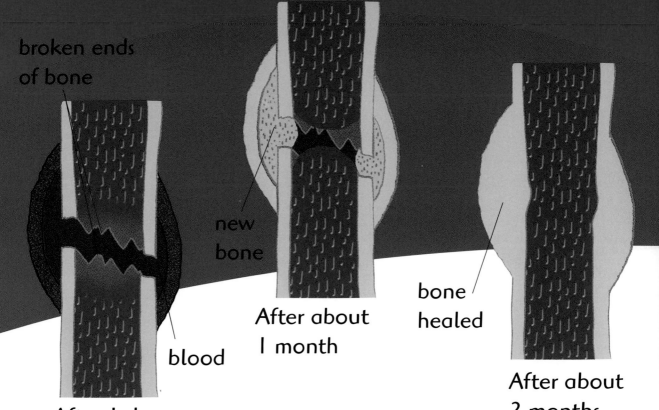

broken ends of bone

new bone

blood

After 1 day

After about 1 month

bone healed

After about 2 months

A broken or cracked **bone heals** itself. Blood closes the break and forms a **clot.** New bone grows slowly between the breaks in the bone.

24

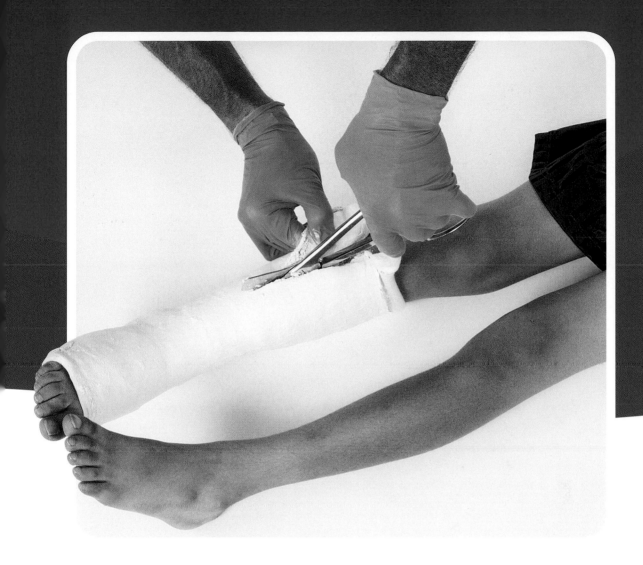

It can take two months or longer until the ends of the bone join and the bone is strong again. Then the **cast** is removed.

Getting Strong Again

After a **cast** is taken off, the **muscles** that move the **joint** are very weak. A **physical therapist** can teach you exercises to make the muscles strong again.

The muscles are weak because you could not use them while the joint was in the cast. You have to do the exercises every day for several weeks to make the muscles strong again.

Preventing Accidents

The best way to not have **accidents** is to be careful! When you are climbing, always move one hand or foot at a time. Do not jump from high places.

Be very careful when you are crossing a street. Cross at safe places, such as traffic lights or **crosswalks.** Look both ways before you cross.

29

Glossary

accident   something that happens by mistake

ankle   joint between your lower leg and your foot

brittle   easily broken

bone   hard material that makes up the skeleton

cast   hard shell that protects a broken bone while it heals

clot   soft lump of thickened blood

concrete   hard substance made from sand, gravel, cement, and water

crosswalk   part of the road marked with black and white stripes where vehicles should stop to let you cross the road

dislocated   out of place

elderly   older person

heal   to mend or become healthy again

injured   hurt or damaged

joint   place where two or more bones meet that allows one bone to move without the other

jolt   sudden shock or hit

ligament   stretchy band that holds a joint together

muscle   part of the body that moves the bones or flesh

physical therapist   person who teaches exercises to help injured or weak muscles become strong

skeleton   all the bones in the body

sprain   when a ligament is damaged by twisting or stretching it too far

X ray   kind of picture that shows the bones inside the body

More Books to Read

Royston, Angela. *Get Some Exercise!*. Chicago: Heinemann Library, 2003.

Royston, Angela. *Safety First*. Chicago: Heinemann Library, 2000.

Royston, Angela. *Why Do Bones Break?: And Other Questions About Movement*. Chicago: Heinemann Library, 2003.

Schaefer, Lola. *Arms, Elbows, Hands, and Fingers*. Chicago: Heinemann Library, 2003.

Index